IN THE FOOTSTEPS OF A THOUSAND GRIEFS

Copyright © 2020 by Wei-Wei Lee
Cover Art by Yvonne Chan

All rights reserved. No part of this publication may be reproduced, distributed, or transmitted in any form or by any means, including photocopying, recording, or other electronic or mechanical methods, without the prior written permission of the author, except in the case of brief quotations embodied in critical reviews and certain other noncommercial uses permitted by copyright law.

The Seattle Youth Poet Laureate is a special program of
Seattle Arts & Lectures in partnership with Urban Word.

ISBN 978-1-949166-03-3

Published by Poetry NW Editions
2000 Tower Street
Everett, WA 98201

Distributed by Ingram

PRINTED IN THE UNITED STATES OF AMERICA

IN THE FOOTSTEPS OF A THOUSAND GRIEFS

Wei-Wei Lee

saudade	1
méiyǔ (plum rain)	2
summer streets	3
開春大吉 (may spring bring fortune)	4
bagung (伯公, in Hakka)	5
jiang zhongwen de hai zhe (the children who speak mandarin)	6
memory scent	7
ahyi	9
fool's gold	11
hello! this is the apocalypse	12
from white terror came us	13
protest in new york	15
patria	16
confessional	17
cold hard marble truth	19
barricade and trebuchet	20
swear down	21
violets	25
et tu	26
storm meets water	26
blue tone	28
tell it to the night	29

finger guns	30
dark room	31
to move heaven	32
cordially	33
floodlands	34
solo	35
solo (ii)	36
construct	37
of and about humanity	38
snapshots	42
weather patterns	43
art, form	44
prepupal stage	45
sundays at seven	46
common room hours	48
ignite	49
three cheers to internet friends	50
our future stands thus	51
Acknowledgements	53
About the Author	55

*speak the words
and see
famine or harvest.
either or.*

saudade

I did not look back.
I did not look back past duty-free
(closing for the night), customs, security, check-in counters,
to see where my father, I thought,
would still be standing, the grumpy old bear
watching his daughter walk away,
before he went out into the black night,
got in his black car,
and drove home alone.

I did not look back until the plane took off,
saw the glow of my city, my homeland, rushing away,
and by then it was too late.

Since then, I am always half-turned, wherever I go.
Into classrooms, turning corners.
On Metro buses or LINK trains.
Walking to school in the soft wash of sun and dew
or headed home, with the chatter of a friend at my side
and cool evening falling.
I keep looking back,
but what I'm looking for isn't there,
won't be there.
Cannot possibly be there.

I look anyway.

Sometimes (a foolish indulgence) when I crest a hill,
I stretch toward the sky on the very tips of my toes,
peering in the direction of the ocean.
If I am tall enough, I think, perhaps I can see
all the way home.
I never do.

méiyǔ (plum rain)

Little me
did not expect
to hold out a hand
amidst the mist
of fine grey drizzle,
long for the crawl
of cars in heavy rain,
the squeak and squeedge
of wipers working overtime
against tides of water,
miss the run to
my mother's car,
sticky-damp even when bone dry,
yelping and hopping
to avoid deceptively shallow puddles
that would soak my shoes and socks
from sole to ankle. A green plum
ripening with the rain.

summer streets

Sweltering, sun scorching.
Cold machine air, burst of chill,
giving way to hot tile.
Your gleam and glow falls narrow
between concrete slabs of building,
too much to love
but sorely missed
when gone. I time
my footsteps to the stream
of harried life, catching
quick gasps of cold air
when doors open and shut.
Hot baking tile, slick and cool
by the time I leave class
this afternoon, I guess,
grey sticky drizzle with the potential
for a downpour.
I itch for that downpour to come down heavy,
to soak me head to toe and chase me
squealing, ducking,
from cover to cover,
banish the heat—
but as I said:
sorely missed when gone.
Year-round under grey sky I miss hot tile
and you, too bright, too much but
loved. I time my footsteps
on crosswalks so I can bask in your gleam,
baking alive and loving it
for a little.

開春大吉 (may spring bring fortune)

lunar new year,
burst of red and
gleam of gold
at every door,
in every hand,
in stitching of my baby coat,
all-call for fortune loud as
the *snap* of firecrackers
just outside
the door.

year of prosperity,
table brimming with
fat pork and saltwater chicken,
whole fish, head 'n tail
with garnish green;
sticky sweet cake
for the following
morning.

prosperity, ring in
with the relatives,
the family friends,
ring in
with sweet oranges
and lacquer fish,
belly-hollow full
of candy.

bagung (伯公, in Hakka)

in my early years, around midday
the old man across the street would
water plants out on the balcony, and I
would holler with all my might.
BAGUNG!

he would startle, look around
his balcony, until his failing eyes land on
the tiny girl across the street,
perched on her grandmother's big wooden desk,
waving madly.

oye, he'd call,
grin splitting his crinkled face,
and wave, slow and languid,
as though we were old friends.

he's getting on in years, now,
getting hard of hearing.
I'm getting older myself, but some little part believes
him to be permanent,
forever watering on the balcony, that
if I scream *bagung* to the waters
the sea and wind will carry it
home for me,
and he will hear.

jiang zhongwen de hai zhe (the children who speak mandarin)

I try to engage. Maybe desperation
has its own tone that rings louder
than my eager voice; you look at me
askew, *maybe*
some other time.
Yes, some other time.
I, too, am familiar
with polite removal, another
common tongue.
Yes, surely, some other time.

That tint to tone, I recognize.
I've heard that
smudge on the words, curling,
your tongue seizing on
strange fickle governing laws where we are
used to other inflections.
I hear it announce
my countrymen.

I try to engage.
Alas, some other time;
you make your excuses, take your
escape, and I sit quiet
with reminiscence
abandoned.

Cue the lone first strains
of anthem.

memory scent

I perk up when I catch the scent,
fifth step on the bridge.
smokeysaltysavory -
sausage!
It's sausage!
Not your bratwurst but our
night market fare,
good Taiwanese pork sausage
grease-shiny over
charcoal grill.

I must be worrying the passersby
with my frantic inhaling, but
what do I care? I am
in the open air, under a swath
of dark sky, velveteen,
if only I close my eyes.

sizzle-crackle.
metal scrapes on metal, brisk
griddles *hiss.*
shwah, shwah!
vendors clamor, their livelihood,
coins rattle
jingle-jingle-clink!
bags are opened with flourish,
plastic rustle and paper snap.
fried dough and fried mushrooms
and fried chicken, our
very best,
bubbling mad in the fryers.
a cacophony of scents and sounds
and all over,
the mouth-watering current
of sausage on the grill.

fifth step on the bridge

the wind shifts;
the smell of sausage, no more than
smoky air touched
by fond memory.
I make my trek to the bus stop hungry,
but not for food.

ahyi

In Mandarin my father's sisters were ever
gugu, gugu; a cheerful cluck of a word
barely dusted off
twice a year.
Ahyi is brighter, more crisp, no less loving;
ahyi for my mother's only sister
whose careful clever hands made
knit blankets and cakes and coffee, planted her own
winding garden,
scaled a fortuitous mulberry tree out in the middle of
absolute nowhere
to bring down the best, blackest berries
for us.

My aunt, my mother's only sister,
ever only *ahyi, ahyi,*
so she has no name.
Not then, and certainly
too late now.

She taught me how to make dumplings. I barely remember
but we went to the market, her and little me,
putt-putting along slow
and then back home.
Wrist-deep in ground pork filling. She
showed me how to
knead out the dumpling dough,
spoon in the filling,
fold it over and close, neat ruffled folds for the edge.
I barely remember
but I curled up on the couch before we were done
with all the rest,
was half-asleep when she came in
to pull a blanket over me
and turn out the lights.

Years later my hands remember the rhythm and routine
better than my memories do:

my dumplings don't fall apart.
She might've taught me more, had we stayed family -
but no, best not dwell
on the memory
of *ahyi*.

fool's gold

the realization that I am the last knot in
a family of unraveling strings
is a cold one.
my parents sleep in their marriage bed, fifteen inches
and a hundred miles apart.
my sister eats at the table with me,
only one, never both,
separated by a year in age
and the bulk of years of silence.
my cousins are getting married, I hear—
from search results, not from my aunt or uncle,
the part of the family that fell out like cookies
crumbling in milk.
I didn't understand the argument then.
I do now
but really, it helps me none.

my friend called me once,
left in the middle of the conversation
to stand, silent spectre, witness to his parents' fight
"couples' spat," he laughed
but we both understood without saying
anything else.
"better than not talking at all," I said
and we both understood that too.

someone's filled the dead air with dry ice.
it smokes and snaps
and no amount of cheer poured over the cracks
fools anyone at all.

hello! this is the apocalypse

they told us
it was coming
when I was only eight,
in the warm breeze of early june,
and poinciana blooming
like flowers set ablaze -

and they told us
every year,
they told us
how to change it,
but we heard the words
when we were helpless
and now it's only
part of our psyche.

they told us
it was coming,
they said
it was too late,
but our slow-cooker death
has been bubbling for decades
and I've only gotten good
at looking away.

from white terror came us

Genetics is such
a sticky thing.
The crooked way I hold my pencils,
the one dinner on the table
that one day back in 2006,
the moss growing deep in my lungs now,
slipperydampfesteringpanic -
every little goddamn thing
marking itself deep
for me, my children,
my great-grandchildren,
and their great-grandchildren.

Don't mess with the code.
My parents, they were born
so many years after
the hush-hush, the nervous looks,
the Orwellian disappearances,
but their parents before them,
they were there.
Those slippery strands of
gossamer fear,
it makes it way into your DNA
and roots there,
curls into some forgotten den
tucked up all cozy
for the winter
and every winter after that.

History and I, our relationship
is fraught with bitter understanding;
we are cursed, for better or worse,
to run along each other
like competing swimmers in neighboring lanes
or like childhood friends racing
for the shore.
Every stroke of my pen,
every up-down of my ribcage

filling and deflating,
has the coal-smudge of
dark history
all over it.

protest in new york

yellow signs with stark black words,
warning colors that catch my eye. I
jerk forward on a pulse beat.
blood calls to blood, after all, and
sunfire runs in all our veins.
the glass is thick with condensation and rain. I
cannot hear, but my bad eyes
see enough.

my people, my people,
people I cannot call
my people
for fear of—

history has wrought in our genes
a withdrawing, a cold deep fear,
a scream to stay uninvolved even if
it breaks our hearts to do so.

no one else knows the language.
calls for me to translate come in quick
but shallow, mere catches of interest.
pulse beat. the crowd beyond the glass, I think,
is yelling.

pulse beat.
I fetch up on the sudden tearing cry
to join them, even as
we drive away.

patria

we don't want for much, me and my mother;
just a name to go by, space to live
we are quiet, me and my mother;
hush, talk musn't be heard.

birds of prey circle.
eyes gleam, hungry, waiting;
my mother turns slowly
and I, young coward, hide in her skirts
sullying silk with wordless tears.
they cannot touch us, says she, confident
(but she watches all the same).

they mean to starve us.
twenty acres, nineteen, then eighteen;
my mother stands stiffly
and I, young coward, hide in her skirts
sullying silk with knowing fear.
they cannot touch us, says she - strained
(even as we lose another).

my mother will die.
blue sky, white sun, ground crimson;
people watch coldly
and I, young coward, hide in her skirts
to *scream.*

gutted, smothered, she says nothing.

we are quiet, me and my mother;
hush, talk musn't be heard
we don't want for much, me and my mother;
just a name to go by, space to live—

—but I suppose that was too much to give.

confessional

My Irene, I imagine, would call me
many names for my
betrayal, hypocrisy, cowardice.
Irene, I'm
~~scared~~
sorry, but this apology
was never meant for you.

Mother. I'm sorry.
A poor way to repay your love in raising
a child of your blood, but I hope

you understand that I'm
~~unworthy~~
scared
to know
what happens to us next, the next
harsh chapter of time,
history the Sisyphean boulder
we can never defeat, please

you know I am
~~a coward~~
always your baby, even if I
dare not say so, even if I
tug my jacket closed to ~~hide~~ protect
the red, white, blue
of your design.

Mother, I am sorry
about your failed daughter.
The best I can do, the best I can do, the best I can

understand, understand, understand,

please.

forgive me.

Irene, you may call
me names, but
call it fear, not shame.

cold hard marble truth

It's a mite hard to believe,
on nights like this
that, somewhere, I have friends who aren't
dream-deep
and snug in their beds, asleep,
but may be dozing off in lecture
with pens stuttering on notes;
air conditioners humming furious
against the peak afternoon heat.
Harder still to believe that while they scribble
and we dream, here,
that someone our age, young and scared
may be learning battle from their own streets,
armed with fury and not much else,
rinsing blood and tear gas
from stinging eyes.

A mite hard to believe, a cold
truth we wish not to know,
that not everyone may be
marveling at the moon
so perfect and lovely,
as I do where I am.

barricade and trebuchet

By the time I say this,
send it out to the world,
we may have our answer,
gods willing,
your people willing,
may it be a happy one.

Your blood of conviction, of fury,
you people of fiercer bone.
We love you for it.
We don't dare say a word,
but through zeros and ones
we are with you, waiting out the storm.

That's the truth of it, isn't it?
Sad quiet truth,
we'd wait out the storm.

You became a storm yourself,
with the screaming winds
to match.

swear down

if we are
made of sun
then perhaps you are
a land of
orchids all.

the news
brings *defiance*.
you are fighting to hold ground
that should be yours, just as
our ground
that should be ours,
and the both of us, in this we
understand.

if you are the trailblazing, skirt-snapping older sister
then we needs must be
the little soldier brother, too green
for a
real fight
but hungry for it,
watching with
wide eyes,
powerless.

and by all the gods that
love us, sister, I swear
we are watching.

cork and bottle your rising spirits. give it to us, to me.
cup our cheek and tell us that
we'll make it through
on fire and fury.

if you had your umbrellas
we had our
lilies and sunflowers
and in this

we
understand that
ground is hard-given.

I pray, if no one else,
by all the gods
that love us,
let us save ourselves.

Take it, this little bit of heart;
I know it isn't much.
But know that in my chest something larger beats
and every inch of it
loves you.

violets

> *all the **violet** tiaras, braided rosebuds, dill and crocus twined around your young neck*
> —Sappho, "By the Time"

I keep coming back to
purple.

In my front yard I grow
velvet-purple violets and ruby-red roses.
They flourish bright and lovely both,
but hardly loved the same.

Such pretty roses!
Such fragrant roses
Wouldn't it be better, really,
if the garden was all roses?

What Strange Violets!
What Queer Violets!
Isn't it unseemly, really,
to even have violets?

What a gorgeous yard of roses!
(There are violets, too.)
My dear, I should think you could tell
your roses from violets.

I grow velvet-purple violets but
I keep them small and hidden.
I tell myself it's for safety;
I tell myself I'm not afraid.

I can tell myself many things.

et tu

A warning. Is that all I am?
A triangular label in blazing yellow
punctuated with an exclamation mark,
like a shriek. An outcry. An
outrage.

She warned my mother, told her
she didn't want me
teaching her son
what I am.

And what am I, exactly?
Am I the little girl you
hugged and taught and
cared for, fed donuts, took shopping for books?
Am I the little girl who
held your son as a toddler,
let him snooze on my lap,
played with him, entertained him,
watched him grow up?
Am I the champion you trained,
were so proud of,
used as a poster child
for years and years and years
and years?

And what are you?
You are the teacher I once looked up to.
You are the mother figure I once adored.
You are the woman who
sealed up all your memories of me
behind protective glass,
slapped a warning label on,
and shepherded your children away.

storm meets water

you haven't moved,
and my sneaky little
tripping fairy feet
spirit away your glass
to refill,
for when you feel that
all too-human burn
of thirst and
come to life like
strings are pulling 'long
your lithe dancer limbs.

your eyes are open but
willing blind.
I open the window
in full
to the first rolling burst
of thunder,
calling on raging
summer storm
to grant us
our next breath

and another.

blue tone

my sister's voice is bleak and blue.
she's telling me that she's exhausted of living
and I sit there with cobalt
seeping down the line and through the screen,
staining our walls, dark.
there's a fear there I can't form.
there's a worry I can't voice.
cobalt envelopes me,
blossoming ink
in water.

ink in water, dyeing thread
so the kids can wear blue shirts to court
like we told 'em to. blue silk tie and
blue cotton shirt, thin-stripe.
they are young and giggly, but sober quick
and give as good as they got. god bless.
have I ever said how proud I am?
my heart expands there, in court on the bench,
opens up to full sky
ever dazzling.

ever dazzling, ever beautiful.
my favorite, that fresh-scrubbed, newly-washed best blue
you'd never notice unless
you take an early morning drive.
pale, pretty silk lightening up from oil-slick midnight,
shade by shade.

tell it to the night

I'm no good at
sadness, as anyone
can tell you.
It splays in my hands like a limp,
sad fish;
my fingers scrabble at nothing,
at air. I can produce
no lifewater.
The best I can do, I'm afraid,
is choke with you,
tripping over useless, common
platitudes. I'm sorry,
but not for the reasons
you would think.

We went driving, the other night,
and I made you trade me your sadness
for mine, or so I told you.
Point by point.
I swallowed my fear, my mounting worry,
my swelling incompetence like a tick
grown fat on blood, ready to burst.
Ironed my voice out smooth,
whipped it light,
gave you the most inane &
innocuous of tales.
Yes, I cheated you. I'm not sorry.
Far be it from me to
make you worry; the reverse, I'm afraid,
is my job.

The second-best I can do, friend,
is trade my strains of happy
for your sorrows,
and bury them shallow
among my own.

fingerguns

it's all gonna turn up, I say.
Fingerguns
to get a smile out of
the crying friend
whose world
has lost gravity.

brace up,
smile, buttercup,
everything's
gonna be okay,
I say, a liar
dredging up
plastic grins

just for them.

dark room

This is where secrets find their rest
in the steady dark, the warmth,
my angels in white shirts
curled up like question marks
against each other.
This is where secrets find their peace
with us, bursting open
on our skin like blisters
being lanced,
lest they swell and fester
and leave a bigger mess.

This is where I lie awake
with my head against your chest,
listening to distinct distant beats—
biting down on secrets
rising in my throat
until I leave teeth marks.

to move heaven

whole swathes of grey
across the sky
like winter air on
your windshield;
I see grey
in your face
as well.

you're sad like the day
is sad, a cloud full of tears.
where is your god up there
somewhere, and what
have you ever done?

dear heart,
poets are mortal, but
for you I'd rip apart
swollen cloud
to show you
blue sky beyond.
for you I would
fight god.

cordially

The poster screams CLIMATE STRIKE /
and a girl wears Vans / in Capitol Hill /
I'm reminded of
you / your smile and laugh / your eyes / your words /
you

if I were smarter / better / smoother / I'd ask you
to go / make a day of it / hold my hand while we shout
for the right / to future

but I'd never risk it / you / your eager heart / mine
quiet never broken / I'd never risk / you / me /
us

floodlands

water bursts over
the grassy banks
of the creek
and I think
I'd like to drown,
but I never.

the hill with
its blinding sentries
casts long shadows,
so I plod home
in the footsteps

of a thousand

griefs.

solo

this house is only
a skeleton now,
the whistle of wind through
cold chimney.

the impress of you
in this space,
now nothing but space,
hollow ring of silence
when I'm alone.

I want the light on
to fill the shadows.

solo (ii)

too much light
in the space where
there used to be
somebody.

construct

destruction is always so
grandiose, but no one
marvels at
construction.

I see tension
in our bridge of
glue and pasta and
hot glue burns on
our tender fingerpads.

I see tension
in steel monsters
painted red and blue and green,
I see welds parting,
metal folding
like wilting flowers
into our
river-veins.

of and about humanity

listen, you with your paper masks, fake blood, rubber hands
you with your scarecrows and ghouls,
pumpkin-headed corpses
—listen, it's people you should fear.

they'll twist your arm, they'll break it clean;
they'll kiss you with poison on blood-smeared teeth.
they'll say sweet words, but have eyes cold;
they'll skin you alive—you'll never be old.
they'll take you apart, delight in their eyes,
and you know when they smile—
they don't sympathize.

imagine, you with your haunted houses, horror flicks, slasher films,
you with your ghosts and goblins,
ruby-eyed demons
—imagine, no imagining, the fear is real—
the monster is in your house.

listen, you with your quiet snow, ombre leaves, rolling seas,
you with your daffodils and daisies,
stripey fat bees
—listen, it's people you should love.

you know them—they've heard your dreams.
held you when you were rending at the seams.
their eyes are soft, their hands are warm;
their words could guide you through a storm.
they'll pull you right in, no need to be shy,
and when they say they love you—
you know they don't lie.

imagine, you with your gold sunsets, blush dawn, silver moon,

you with your fields and meadows,
star-spattered sky
—imagine, no imagining, nothing to fear—
the angels are by your side.

*It's a strange thing to know that you're loved.
A foreign concept, but these, surely,
are foreign lands.*

snapshots

three triumphant beaming faces, three cans of silly string.
three people around my table; cake and candle-glow.
grins and laughter, card games
and wings of whipped cream
for that certain *je ne sais quoi*.
zoom in, focus.
click-click.
what a luxury it is
to be loved.

black night, streetlights;
squint and you could be anywhere.
the roads are empty and my father's
car of fifteen has its whine.
Its driver is fifty over
but came to collect his daughter
anyway.
no focus. click-click.
flying away, again and again.

today: sunroof open, driving fast
there and back.
across a coffee table, bright eyes and bright minds.
a pair of voices overlapping, gifting me words
I don't see and maybe never will.
until then, though -
"you didn't take notes?" one laughs. "we'll repeat it."
smiles.
zoom in. focus.
thank you.

weather patterns

the lady in the elevator called,
"look at that rainbow!"
and we all did,
sticking our necks out past the doors to get a
good look.
we are so starved for pretty things.

but there was no rainbow,
only the faintest smudge of purple
against the cotton fluff of clouds
spread across the sky like quilt batting,
blocking out most of the
fresh-washed sky
as pale and clean
as first light.

I looked back at her,
the lady in the elevator,
and her eyes, so wide and wondering
and delighted
about that bare smear of color
in the sky.

if I've seen better rainbows,
that is my joy to have.

"it's beautiful," I say, and she beams —
and there, in the curve of her smile,
I see what she means.

art, form

We are vibrant pieces forming
a more splendid picture,
no fragment too small
for our blank corners.
We are mere threads alone,
but woven, we become
a marvel.

We are never ugly, only seen
from different angles.
We are better shown
in collection,
together.

Let us be a pencil sketch
on leftover butcher paper,
white canvas painted
with white strokes.
Let us be shattered pottery
mended with gold
and fluid twisting sculptures
gleaming with chrome.

Above all,
let us be known.

prepupal stage

I am alive but barely living,
won't you have mercy? go on;
tug my shoulder free,
one after the other,
the frost-husk of me shedding—
onto the second prepupal stage,
fly away,
gone.

I am alive, I am awake,
this cold expanse,
I hear ringing things that just aren't there,
won't you have mercy? go on;
draw up the string through my head
and pull me into function,
marionette,
keep me going.

I am alive but do I dream?
These words aren't even mine.
Am I my own
possession?

sundays at seven

Sunday mornings rising.
Not of the faith, never been to church,
but here I am in the biting air
like a street vendor with a cotton candy cart; my breaths
spun-sugar white.
They pull up with no announcement, no fanfare—
faces turned, expecting, though.
Here we are; off we go.

No people on the roads. We go fast
under the speed limit.
Music croons, backdrop to bickering laughter born of
the chaos of familiarity, or maybe
the familiarity of chaos.

The streetlights could look like stars.

Caffeine is bought and the table we frequent is
empty and waiting for
its wayward guests.
We are armed with determination and
resignation. We come knowing
there is work to be done.

Unsure. We are too young to be
where we are and our footing
too precarious, too often.
If I am but human amongst
the best of us and the best of us
are tired,
where do we go from there?

The wood grain swirls like currents
pulling us downstream.

Drink from the flood, or let the flood
drown you.

Religion holds no sway on Sundays,
but my silent prayer offered to gods across an ocean
as we file back out to a lighter sky and roads
more lively, though we still don't slow
on the way home,
surely gives the ones I love
what little blessing I can.

common room hours

We are the sticky raw emotion
that seeps into honey-wood wall
and the dusky sky above
touched starless, endless
expanse seeing all of us
to bed, parting clumps turning
single-cell and lonely
but never quite alone.
We are the sconces, white wax light,
and stretching golden windows.
We are so much blue.
We are pale stone buildings, pale stone walk,
the kids who seeped into the woodwork and carvings,
leaving marks to be found years later:
we were here, were here, were here.

ignite

the night is young
our youth kindling, our bones to smoke
powder clouds bursting into nebulae
our screams echo under the sky
alight with light and heat
we shall surely die
but tonight
we are dancing, wild things
burn like comets and crash as hard
we are on fire.

three cheers to internet friends

I've wondered about you
for years and years
and I hope this reaches you,
wherever you are:
that I love and miss you,
that I never forgot you,
that wherever we are
in the world now, our
pulled apart taffy-sticky
way back when,
we knew the first forms of each other
at least a little bit.

and you I've known
for years and years
and there's not much talk now, but
it's the kind of content quiet silence
that comes easy from
two people who know each other
well enough to make
the radio silence just a lull
in conversation.
a long lull. we don't mind.
it's enough to know
we exist.

last toast to you,
and I've never met you
but maybe I will
or maybe I won't.
whichever way, there comes
a steadiness in knowing
that someone else
has both feet on the ground,
may be walking and talking and joking
on the same patch of land that stretches
coast to coast.

our future stands thus

I think our future lies in those
in classrooms, clutching
binderfuls of paper
and looking like death
warmed over, true;
but present,
awake and alive,
each generation more willing to
voice darker stories,
like tilling soil over
for new seed.

I see our future alive and well and
present in those in front of me,
the ones we train and raise
ourselves,
the pinpricks of light that come together
before the threshold, on the precipice,
to become supernovas.

When I see you dressed and suited,
I see you solemn—
I see you as planets with gravitational pull.
Changing, by little, the fabric of the universe,
shaping who we are,
what we are,
who we become.

Acknowledgements

First and foremost, thank you to the ancestors who have seen me across the water into foreign lands, and to Taiwan, the land that raised me. I hope I have given you reason to be proud. I hope I have brought you honor.

Thank you to Matt Gano and Aaron Counts for teaching me how to hone my writing and, most of all, to trust it. It has been an honor to learn from you both. Thank you to the fabulous Bre'Anna Girdy and Alicia Craven, who have performed Herculean feats of organization, and to the brilliant folks at Seattle Arts and Lectures and Poetry Northwest. This book would not have been possible without any of you.

To all my friends: The beauty of you, your warmth and kindness, your trust, your humor, your infinite chaos and love—it inspires me every day. Thank you. I love you.

Thank you to the literary circles of Nathan Hale High School, and Nathan Hale High School itself, for welcoming me with open arms and giving me a place in your communities. Thank you to Seattle, my second home. You have shown me kindness and given me opportunity beyond my wildest dreams. You never cease to amaze me.

Last but never least, to Doug Sylver, who sacrificed his lunch periods so I could rehearse and came to all my readings, who has shown pride in me and given me his unwavering support. In my native Mandarin, so goes the proverb, 天涯海角有盡處, 只有師恩無窮期。There are boundaries to the world beyond, but the grace of a teacher is boundless. Thank you.

About the Author

Wei-Wei Lee is eighteen years old and attends Nathan Hale High School. She grew up in Taiwan, but was born in the States, and Seattle is the first city in the States she has ever known and loved. As the 2019/2020 Youth Poet Laureate, she hopes to pay tribute to both Taiwan and America in her writing, and she hopes to do them proud.

This book is set in Sabon, Floane, and LFT Etica
Book design by Cara Sutherland with assistance from
Bre'Anna Girdy and Abi Pollokoff

Produced and published by Poetry NW Editions,
an educational press in the Written Arts Program
at Everett Community College,
with the assistance of editorial interns
Sophie Campo, Avery Ramuta, and Michelle Storer

www.ingramcontent.com/pod-product-compliance
Lightning Source LLC
Chambersburg PA
CBHW030201100526
44592CB00009B/384